California Fish Species

Game Fish & Panfish

Billy Grinslott & Kinsey Marie Books

ISBN - 9781968228231

Sculpins are small, bottom-dwelling fish with a flattened body shape, large pectoral fins, and a unique camouflage pattern, often found in clear, fast-flowing waters with rocky substrates, and they are known for their ambush hunting tactics. Sculpins have very large mouths and can swallow items nearly as large as themselves.

The Green Sunfish is blue green in color. It has yellow flecks on both its scales and some parts of its sides. The Green Sunfish also has broken blue stripes which is why some people confuse it with the Bluegill. Green Sunfish are very adaptable. They can live in any body of water that has vegetation or weeds. Green sunfish are opportunistic feeders, consuming insects, small fish, crayfish, and other invertebrates.

The bluegill also considered a sunfish is the most popular fish to fish for. They are called pan fish because they are about the size of a frying pan. Bluegills love to eat insects and bugs. They have good vision and rely on their keen eyesight to feed. Three types in this group are the Bluegill, Sunfish, and Pumpkinseed.

The Warmouth is a member of the Rock Bass, Green Sunfish and Bluegill family. They can survive in low oxygen environments while other fish cannot. Warmouth can thrive in muddy water, when other fish can't. Warmouth are often confused with rock bass. The difference between the two is in the anal fin: warmouth have three spines on the anal fin ray and rock bass have six spines.

Redear sunfish are known for their red or orange-edged gill flaps. They are a type of sunfish that thrive in warm, quiet waters, feeding primarily on mollusks and snails, and can grow up to 12 inches and weigh as much as 2 pounds. They are also known as shellcracker, due to their diet and the way they crush shells. The redear sunfish will thrive in most warm-water lakes and streams.

The Pumpkinseed is also known as pond perch, sun perch, and punky's sunfish. It can be found in numerous lakes, ponds, and rivers. It is their body shape resembling the seed of a pumpkin, that inspired their name. Pumpkinseed sunfish have speckles on their orangish colored sides and back, with a yellow to orange belly and chest. They are active during the day and rest at night near the bottom or in shelter areas.

Sucker fish, also known as suckers, are freshwater fish with a unique sucker shaped mouth on the underside of their head. There are several types of sucker fish. Sucker fish feed off the bottom with their suction cup shaped mouth. The Nevada state record for a mountain sucker is 5 pounds, 2 ounces, and 21 inches long.

There are two main types of crappies. The white crappie and the black crappie. They are also members of the sunfish family. The difference between the white and black crappie is one has dark spots and the other has dark lines and is lighter in color. The white crappie has six dorsal fin spines, whereas the black crappie has eight dorsal fin spines. The white crappie can grow bigger and more of the bigger white crappie are caught in North America.

Whitefish are related to salmon and trout. They are known for their deep-bodied, silvery appearance and are a major part of a lake's ecosystem. They typically grow to 17-22 inches and range from 1.5 to 4 pounds. Whitefish are a popular and valuable commercial fish, generating income for commercial fisheries. Whitefish are also known as, whiting, and shad. The Nevada state record for Mountain Whitefish is 4 pounds.

Gizzard shad typically grow to lengths between 9 and 14 inches, but some can reach over 20 inches, with a record specimen weighing in at 2.97 pounds. Gizzard shad, introduced as a forage fish, are now found in large rivers, lakes, and reservoirs. Gizzard shad are primarily nocturnal. The American gizzard shad also known as the mud shad, is a member of the herring family of fish. The gizzard shad is named for its muscular, gizzard-like stomach.

Despite the name, Sacramento perch belong to the sunfish family, not the perch family. They have brown backs and sides, often with a metallic green to purplish sheen, and 6-7 irregular vertical bars on their sides. Adults typically average 0.5-2 pounds in weight but can reach sizes exceeding 3 pounds. They prefer sluggish, heavily vegetated waters of sloughs and lakes, but can also be found in rivers, floodplains, and estuaries.

The two most famous perches are the common perch and the yellow perch. The yellow perch has a brilliant greenish yellow color with orange fins. The yellow perch is the biggest one and can grow to a size of 18 inches. It's also known as the jumbo perch. The other type of perch is the white perch. The current Nevada state record for yellow perch is 1 pound 9 ounces.

The black bullhead and yellow bullhead are part of the catfish family. They usually only grow to about 10 inches long. They use their whiskers to help find food. The bullhead is the most common member of the catfish family. Bullheads live in the water containing low oxygen levels. They can survive on low oxygen areas, where other fish can't.

White catfish are interesting because they are smaller than other common catfish species like channel catfish, they have a wider head and lack the black spots of channel catfish. White catfish are the smallest of the large North American catfish species. The White catfish has white chin barbells, which distinguish it from other species. There are four pairs of barbels, whiskers around the mouth, two on the chin, one at the angle of the mouth, and one behind the nostril. The largest White catfish caught in Nevada is 17 pounds, 4 ounces.

Flathead Catfish, their body is wide but flattened and very low in height. Both eyes are on the top of the flattened head, giving excellent vision to see upward. Flathead catfish live mainly in large bodies of water like big rivers and reservoirs. They prefer deep pools of water. The largest Flathead Catfish caught in Nevada was a 95-pound fish.

The Channel Catfish are the most fished catfish species with around 8 million anglers fishing for them per year. Channel Catfish have very few teeth and swallow their food whole. Channel catfish live in freshwater rivers, lakes, streams, and ponds. Catfish can live in low oxygen water, like bullheads. The largest Channel Catfish caught in Kentucky weighed 32 pounds.

There are several species of catfish. Blue catfish are known for their size, reaching over 100 pounds. Blue catfish, like other catfish, lack scales and have smooth skin. They have barbels (whiskers) around their mouths, which are used for sensing and tasting food. They are generally slate blue on the back and silvery/white on the underside. The largest blue catfish ever caught in Kentucky weighed 106.9 pounds.

Carp have long been an important food fish to humans. Carp are bottom feeders for the most part and their mouth is made like a suction cup, so they can suck food off the bottom. Carp are good for a lake because they help clean the bottom of the lake. Carp can tolerate a wide range of water temperatures and low oxygen levels, allowing them to survive in a variety of habitats. Carp are considered an invasive species in many areas. The largest carp caught in Nevada was a 35-pound, 3-ounce fish.

White Bass range in color from a silvery white to a pale green. Their backs are mostly black, while their sides and belly are pale with stripes running along them. White Bass are related to Striped Bass and also called wipers. The Nevada state record for White Bass in Nevada is 4 pounds.

Striped bass are often called Stripers. Striped bass live in both salt and fresh water. Striped bass have very sensitive eyes and will seek deep water when the sun is out. Striped bass have a preferred water temperature range of from 55° F to 68° F, and swim to find water of these temperatures. White Bass are related to Striped Bass and have lighter stripes on their sides. The largest striped bass caught in Nevada, which holds the state record, weighed 63 pounds.

The largemouth bass is the most sought-after bass in North America. Largemouth bass live in just about every lake in North America. They have great hearing and can hear a crayfish crawling on the bottom of the lake. Largemouth are also found in many of the same bodies of water as smallmouth bass. The largest largemouth bass caught in Nevada weighed 12 pounds.

Smallmouth bass have a smaller mouth than the largemouth bass. They also have different markings and are lighter in color. They prefer living in colder water. Smallmouth bass prefer clear, cool waters with rocky or gravel bottoms in lakes, rivers, and streams. The current world record smallmouth is an 11-pound, 15-ounce fish caught in Dale Hollow Lake. The largest Smallmouth bass caught in Nevada was an 8-pound, 11-ounces. It measured 21.5 inches long.

Spotted bass have rows of dark spots on their sides and an iridescent green pattern along their back. Spotted bass are also known as Kentucky's or redeye bass. They are a popular game fish, often mistaken for largemouth bass, but they have subtle differences like a a smaller mouth. They are known for their aggressive nature and tendency to school together. They also prefer rocky bottoms and being in deeper water compared to other bass who like shallow water. The Nevada state record for a spotted bass is 4 pounds, 2 ounces.

Pikeminnows are voracious predators, consuming millions of young salmon and steelhead annually in the river systems. They can live at least 11 years. Pikeminnows are known for their aggressive feeding habits, consuming fish, invertebrates, and even terrestrial insects. While lacking teeth, pikeminnows are still impressive predators, utilizing their strong bodies and powerful tails to capture prey.

Sturgeons have sharp spines on their back, so be careful when handling them. Instead of scales, sturgeon skin is covered in bony plates called scutes, which can be very sharp on young sturgeon. Sturgeons have been around since the dinosaur days. Sturgeons mostly live in large, freshwater lakes and rivers. Their average lifespan is 50 to 100 years. The largest sturgeon in North America, a white sturgeon, weighed 1,102.3 pounds.

Redband trout are a subspecies of native rainbow trout that have adapted to a variety of freshwater habitats. Redband trout are known to grow larger than typical rainbow trout, with some fish reaching lengths over 24 inches. Some Redband trout are anadromous (migrate to the ocean) and are known as Redband steelhead. The largest Redband trout caught in Oregon, was 34 inches and weighed 25 pounds.

Chinook also known as the king salmon are the most widespread Salmon in North America. Chinook salmon are hatch in freshwater streams and rivers then migrate out to the saltwater environment of the ocean to feed and grow. Chinook salmon are the largest of the Pacific Ocean salmon, that's how they got the name king salmon. The Oregon record for a Chinook salmon is 83 pounds.

Brook trout are characterized by their olive-green bodies with pale, worm-like markings, red spots with bluish halos, and orange-red fins with white and black edges. They can grow up to 12 inches in length. Brook trout are cold-water fish that prefer clean, clear, and cold streams, lakes, and ponds. The Nevada state record Brook trout is 5 pounds.

Coho salmon, also known as silver salmon, are fish that live in both freshwater and saltwater, migrating from the ocean to their natal streams to spawn, where they die shortly after. Some coho salmon migrate more than 1,000 miles in the ocean, while others remain in marine areas close to the streams where they were born. Adult coho salmon typically weigh 8 to 12 pounds and are 24 to 30 inches long, but some can reach up to 36 pounds. The largest Coho salmon caught in Oregon weighed 25 pounds 5 ounces.

Brown trout can live up to 20 years. Brown trout have higher tolerance for warmer waters than either brook or rainbow trout. Brown trout can be found on almost every continent except Antarctica, and many can be found living in the ocean. The Nevada state record for brown trout is 27 pounds, 5 ounces.

Chum salmon, also known as dog salmon, are a common Pacific salmon species. They are the most widely distributed of all Pacific salmon species, found in coastal streams from Arctic Alaska to San Diego, California. Chum salmon have a dark olive-green back and dark maroon sides, with irregular greenish vertical bars on the sides, and no spots on the back or tail. Chum salmon are medium-sized fish, averaging 24 inches in length and between 9.7 to 22 lbs. in weight. The largest Chum salmon caught in Oregon weighed 23 pounds.

The cutthroat's name comes from the bright red or orange slash-like markings under their jaws. There are several subspecies of cutthroat trout, including the Lahontan cutthroat trout and Paiute cutthroat trout They inhabit a variety of cold, freshwater environments, including small streams, rivers, and lakes. Mature cutthroat trout can range from 6 to 40 inches in length. The largest cutthroat trout ever caught in Nevada was a 41-pound Lahontan Cutthroat Trout.

Tiger trout are known for their aggressive nature and awesome looking tiger-like stripes. Tiger trout are not naturally occurring in the wild, but rather a hybrid created by mixing a female brown trout with a male brook trout. They are stocked in lakes and rivers. Their striking appearance with tiger-like stripes and patterns, makes them easily recognizable. They are known to grow faster than their parent species. The unofficial state record for a tiger trout in Nevada is a 20-pound, 4-ounce fish.

The rainbow trout gets its name because of its brilliant colors. Rainbow trout populations are good indicators of water pollution because they can only survive in clean waters. They like to live in rivers and streams. Rainbow trout rank among the top five most sought game fish in North America. The Nevada state record for rainbow trout is a 16-pound, 8-ounce fish, 30.5 inches long.

Mature Golden trout have a deep olive-green back that fades to bright gold on the sides, a vibrant red-orange lateral line, and black speckles near the tail. Golden trout are native to the remote waters at elevations of 6,000 to 10,000 feet. Golden trout, typically average 6 to 12 inches in length. The largest Golden trout caught in Nevada weighed 6 pounds.

The lake trout known as Mackinaw is one of the biggest of the trout family. The biggest lake trout caught was 72 pounds. Lake trout like to live in lakes that are deep. They like being in the cool water in the deep parts of a lake. They have been reported to live up to 70 years in some Canadian lakes. They are native to North America. The largest lake or Mackinaw trout caught in Nevada weighed 37 pounds and 6 ounces. was 44 inches long.

The primary salmon species you'll find are landlocked sockeye salmon, also known as kokanee. These are the non-anadromous form of sockeye salmon, meaning they don't migrate to the ocean. They live their entire lives in freshwater lakes and reservoirs. The state record for Kokanee salmon in Nevada weighed 5 pounds, 2 ounces.

Fun Facts About California Fish

1 - California has two state fish: the California Golden Trout (freshwater) and the Garibaldi (marine).

2 - The Lahontan cutthroat trout, is the largest inland cutthroat trout in the world

3 - The pikeminnow is the largest minnow species, growing up to six feet long and weighing over 80 pounds.

4 - There are 125 species of freshwater fish in California. This includes 67 native species, 53 non-native species.

5 - The largest freshwater fish ever caught in California is the White Sturgeon, with the world record being a 468-pound fish.

6 - The smallest freshwater fish species in California is likely the Delta Smelt, which typically reaches about 2.4-2.8 inches and a maximum size of about 4.7 inches.

7 - In California, some of the most commonly caught freshwater fish species include largemouth bass, rainbow trout, channel catfish, and common carp.

Author Page

Billy Grinslott & Kinsey Marie Books

Copyright, All Rights Reserved

ISBN – 9781968228231

Thanks